FATS AND SUGARS

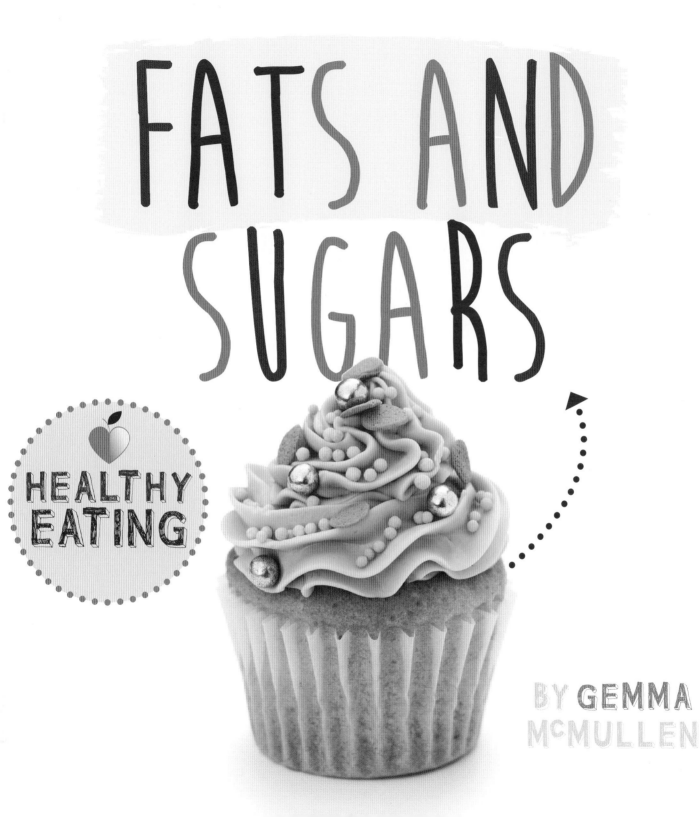

HEALTHY EATING

BY GEMMA McMULLEN

CONTENTS

Look out for the underlined words in this book, they are explained in the glossary on page 24.

©2016
Book Life
King's Lynn
Norfolk PE30 4LS

ISBN: 978-1-910512-45-6

Written by:
Gemma McMullen
Edited by:
Grace Jones
Designed by:
Ian McMullen

A catalogue record for this book
is available from the British Library.

WHAT ARE FATS AND SUGARS?

Fat is an important part of our diet. Our bodies need small amounts of fat. We eat fats from animals and plants. We also use fats in our cooking.

Sausages contain animal fat.

Sugar is a sweet substance which comes from plants.
It is used to make food and drinks taste nice.

White Sugar
Cubes

ANIMAL FATS

Sometimes, we cook and eat animal fat. Bacon rind is fat. Some meats contain more fats than others.

Fatty Part of Meat.

Bacon

Animal fat is also used inside food products. It can be found in some products where you might not expect it to be in.

Crisps

Chocolate

Jelly

Sweets

Vegetarians need to be careful when choosing what to eat, because they may be eating animal fats.

COOKING OILS

Sometimes, we use fats to cook other foods in. Cooking food in oil is called frying. We can also use oil as an ingredient.

Cooking oils can be made from plants. Sunflower oil and olive oil are both used in many homes to cook with.

Sometimes oil is poured onto food, such as salad.

BUTTER, LARD AND MARGARINE

Butter is a dairy product because it is made from milk. Butter is also used as a fat for cooking because it is made using butterfat.

Butter

Lard is a fat which comes from pigs. Margarine is made using sunflower oil. It contains less fat than butter and lard.

Margarine

Lard

HEALTHY FATS

We need fats in our diets to keep us healthy. Fats give us energy and keep our skin and organs healthy. Fish, nuts, fruit and vegetables all contain healthy fats.

Healthy fats such as fish, nuts and fruit give us energy.

Too much fat in our diets can make us overweight. It is important to think about the amount of fat we eat.

Biscuits

Biscuits and pastries both contain fat.

Pastries

WHERE DOES SUGAR COME FROM?

Sugar comes from sugar cane or sugar beet.

Sugar Cane

Sugar cane is a grass which grows in warm climates with heavy downpours of rain.

Sugar beet is a root vegetable which grows in countries with cooler climates, such as in Europe.

Sugar Beet

HEALTHY SUGARS

Some sugar in our diet is good because it gives us energy. Natural sugars such as those in fruit are better for us than added sugars.

Food which has sugar added to it is not as good for us and should only be eaten as a treat.

Too much sugar is bad news for our teeth.

HIDDEN SUGARS

We know that there is a lot of sugar in sweets and fizzy drinks, but some foods contain hidden sugars that we might not know about.

Dried fruit contains sugars

Too much sugar can make us overweight.

Even savoury foods such as soups contain sugar. Flavoured yoghurt, pasta sauce and even dried fruits all have sugar added to them.

TYPES OF SUGAR

Granulated sugar is the sugar that is most used. It is used in baking and to make hot drinks sweeter.

Granulated

Caster

Caster sugar contains very small pieces of sugar. It is good for making cakes.

Sanding sugar is mainly used for decorating sweet foods. Its crystals are very large.

Muscovado

Muscovado sugar feels sandy, sticky and wet. It is brown in colour and can be used to sweeten coffee.

21

FOODY FACTS!

The avocado is a fruit which is high in fat.

Jam

Sugar helps to keep food fresh for longer.